Liturgy of the Reformed Churches of the Netherlands

By

Reformed Churches of the Netherlands

First published in 1944

Published by Left of Brain Books

Copyright © 2023 Left of Brain Books

ISBN 978-1-397-66890-5

First Edition

All rights reserved. No part of this publication may be reproduced, distributed, or transmitted in any form or by any means, including photocopying, recording, or other electronic or mechanical methods, without the prior written permission of the publisher, except in the case of brief quotations permitted by copyright law. Left of Brain Books is a division of Left Of Brain Onboarding Pty Ltd.

PUBLISHER'S PREFACE

About the Book

"The Reformed Churches in the Netherlands (Liberated) (Dutch: Gereformeerde Kerken in Nederland (vrijgemaakt)) are a Protestant denomination that holds to an orthodox view of Neo-Calvinist doctrine. The church arose in 1944 out of the so-called Liberation (Vrijmaking), when it separated from the Reformed Churches in the Netherlands. Prof. Dr. Klaas Schilder played an important role in the Liberation. There are currently 270 affiliated local congregations with a total of 125,905 members."

(Quote from wikipedia.org)

CONTENTS

PUBLISHER'S PREFACE
FORM FOR THE ADMINISTRATION OF BAPTISM 1
FORM FOR THE PUBLIC CONFESSION OF FAITH 9
FORM FOR THE PUBLIC CONFESSION OF GUILT 10
FORM FOR THE ADMINISTRATION OF THE LORD'S SUPPER 11
FORM OF EXCOMMUNICATION 21
FORM OF READMITTING EXCOMMUNICATED PERSONS 25
FORM OF ORDINATION OF THE MINISTERS OF GOD'S WORD ... 29
FORM OF ORDINATION OF ELDERS AND DEACONS 36
FORM FOR THE INSTALLATION OF PROFESSORS OF THEOLOGY 43
FORM OR ORDINATION OF MISSIONARIES 47
FORM FOR THE CONFIRMATION OF MARRIAGE BEFORE THE CHURCH 54

FORM FOR THE ADMINISTRATION OF BAPTISM

THE principal parts of the doctrine of holy baptism are these three:

First. That we with our children are conceived and born in sin, and therefore are children of wrath, in so much that we cannot enter into the kingdom of God, except we are born again. This, the dipping in, or sprinkling with water teaches us, whereby the impurity of our souls is signified, and we admonished to loathe, and humble ourselves before God, and seek for our purification and salvation without ourselves.

Secondly. Holy baptism witnesses and seals unto us the washing away of our sins through Jesus Christ. Therefore we are baptized in the name of the Father, and of the Son, and of the Holy Ghost. For when we are baptized in the name of the Father, God the Father witnesses and seals unto us, that he does make an eternal covenant of grace with us, and adopts us for his children and heirs, and therefore will provide us with every good thing, and avert all evil or turn it to our profit. And when we are baptized in the name of the Son, the Son seals unto us, that he does wash us in his blood from all our sins, incorporating us into the fellowship of his death and resurrection, so that we are freed from all our sins, and accounted righteous before God. In like manner, when we are baptized in the name of the Holy Ghost, the Holy Ghost assures us, by this holy sacrament, that he will dwell in us, and sanctify us to be members of Christ, applying unto us, that which we have in Christ, namely, the washing away of our sins, and the daily renewing of our lives, till we shall finally be presented without spot or wrinkle among the assembly of the elect in life eternal.

Thirdly. Whereas in all covenants, there are contained two parts: therefore are we by God through baptism, admonished of, and obliged unto new obedience, namely, that we cleave to this one God, Father, Son, and Holy Ghost; that we trust in him, and love him with all our hearts, with all our souls, with all our mind, and with all our strength; that we forsake the world, crucify our old nature, and walk in a new and holy life. And if we sometimes through weakness fall into sin, we must not therefore despair of God's mercy, nor continue in sin, since baptism is a seal and undoubted testimony, that we have an eternal covenant of grace with God.

1. To Infants of Believers

And although our young children do not understand these things, we may not therefore exclude them from baptism, for as they are without their knowledge, partakers of the condemnation in Adam, so are they again received unto grace in Christ; as God speaks unto Abraham, the father of all the faithful, and therefore unto us and our children (Gen. 17:7), saying, "I will establish my covenant between me and thee, and thy seed after thee, in their generations, for an everlasting covenant; to be a God unto thee, and to thy seed after thee." This also the Apostle Peter testifies, with these words (Acts 2:39), "For the promise is unto you and to your children, and to all that are afar off, even as many as the Lord our God shall call." Therefore God formerly commanded them to be circumcised, which was a seal of the covenant, and of the righteousness of faith; and therefore Christ also embraced them, laid his hands upon them and blessed them (Mark 10).

Since then baptism is come in the place of circumcision, therefore infants are to be baptized as heirs of the kingdom of God, and of his covenant. And parents are in duty bound, further to instruct their children herein, when they shall arrive to years of discretion.

That therefore this holy ordinance of God may be administered to his glory, to our comfort, and to the edification of his Church, let us call upon his holy name.

Prayer

O Almighty and eternal God, Thou, who hast according to thy severe judgment punished the unbelieving and unrepentant world with the flood, and hast according to thy great mercy saved and protected believing Noah and his family; Thou, who hast drowned the obstinate Pharaoh and his host in the Red Sea, and hast led thy people Israel through the midst of the Sea upon dry ground, by which baptism was signified - we beseech thee, that Thou wilt be pleased of thine infinite mercy, graciously to look upon these children, and incorporate them by thy Holy Spirit, into thy Son Jesus Christ, that they may be buried with him into his death, and be raised with him in newness of life; that they may daily follow him, joyfully bearing their cross, and cleave unto him in true faith, firm hope, and ardent love; that they may, with a comfortable sense of thy favour, leave this life, which is nothing but a continual death, and at the last day, may appear without terror before the judgment seat of Christ thy Son, through Jesus Christ our Lord, who with thee and the Holy Ghost, one only God, lives and reigns forever. Amen.

An exhortation to the Parents

Beloved in the Lord Jesus Christ, you have heard that baptism is an ordinance of God, to seal unto us and to our seed his covenant; therefore it must be used for that end, and not out of custom or superstition. That it may then be manifest, that you are thus minded, you are to answer sincerely to these questions:

First, Whether you acknowledge, that although our children are conceived and born in sin, and therefore are subject to all miseries, yea, to condemnation itself; yet that they are sanctified in Christ, and therefore, as members of his Church ought to be baptized?

Secondly. Whether you acknowledge the doctrine which is contained in the Old and New Testament, and in the articles of the Christian faith, and which is taught here in this Christian Church, to be the true and perfects doctrine of salvation?

Thirdly. Whether you promise and intend to see these children, when come to the years of discretion (whereof you are either parent or witness), instructed and brought up in the aforesaid doctrine, or help or cause them to be instructed therein, to the utmost of your power?

Answer. Yes.

Then the Minister of God's Word, in baptizing, shall say, I baptize thee in the name of the Father, and of the Son, and of the Holy Ghost. Amen.

Thanksgiving

Almighty God and merciful Father, we thank and praise thee, that Thou hast forgiven us, and our children, all our sins, through the blood of thy beloved Son Jesus Christ, and received us through thy Holy Spirit as members of thine only begotten Son, and adopted us to be thy children, and sealed and confirmed the same unto us by holy baptism; we beseech thee, through the same Son of thy love, that Thou wilt be pleased always to govern these baptized children by Thy Holy Spirit, that they may be piously and religiously educated, increase and grow up in the Lord Jesus Christ, that they then may acknowledge thy fatherly goodness and mercy, which Thou hast shown to them and us, and live in all righteousness, under our only Teacher, King and High Priest, Jesus Christ; and manfully fight against, and overcome sin, the devil and his whole dominion, to the end that they may eternally praise and magnify thee, and thy Son Jesus Christ, together with the Holy Ghost, the one only true God. Amen.

2. To Adult Persons

However children of Christian parents (although they understand not this mystery) must be baptized by virtue of the covenant; yet it is not lawful to baptize those who are come to years of discretion, except they first be sensible of their sins, and make confession both of their repentance and faith in Christ. For this cause did not only John the Baptist preach (according to the command of God) the baptism of repentance, and baptized, for the remission of sins, those who confessed their sins (Mark 1 and Luke 3); but our Lord Jesus Christ also commanded his disciples to teach all nations, and then to baptize them, in the name of the Father, and of the Son, and of the Holy Ghost (Matt. 28, Mark 16), adding this promise: "He that believeth and is baptized shall be saved". According to which rule, the Apostles, as appears from Acts 2, 10 and 16, baptized none who were of years of discretions, but such as made confession of their faith and repentance. Therefore it is not lawful now to baptize any other adult person, than such as have been taught the mysteries of holy baptism, by the preaching of the gospel, and are able to give an account of their faith by the confession of the mouth.

That therefore this holy ordinance of God may be administered to his glory, to our comfort, and to the edification of his Church, let us call upon his holy name:

O Almighty and eternal God, Thou, who hast according to thy severe judgment punished the unbelieving and unrepentant world with the flood, and hast according to thy great mercy saved and protected believing Noah and his family; Thou, who hast drowned the obstinate Pharaoh and his host in the Red Sea, and hast led thy people Israel through the midst of the Sea upon dry ground, by which baptism is signified - we beseech thee, that Thou wilt be pleased of thine infinite mercy, graciously to look upon this person, and incorporate him by thy Holy Spirit into thy Son Jesus Christ, that he may be buried with him into his death, and be raised with him in newness of life; that he may daily follow him, joyfully bearing his cross, and cleave unto him in true faith, firm hope, and ardent love; that he may with a comfortable sense of thy favour, leave this life, which is nothing but a continual death, and at the last day, may appear without terror before the judgment seat of Christ thy Son, through Jesus Christ our Lord, who with thee and the Holy Ghost, one only God, lives and reigns forever. Amen.

Since therefore thou, are also desirous of holy baptism, to the end, that it may be to thee a seal of thine ingrafting into the Church of God; that it may appear that thou do not only receive the Christian religion, in which thou have been privately instructed by us and of which also thou have made confession before us, but that thou (through the grace of God), intends and purposes to lead a life according to the same, thou are sincerely to give answer before God and his Church.

First. Do thou believe in the only true God, distinct in three persons, Father, Son, and Holy Ghost, who has made heaven and earth, and all that in them is, of nothing, and still maintains and governs them, insomuch that nothing comes to pass, either in heaven or on earth, without his divine will?

Answer. Yes.

Secondly. Do thou believe that thou are conceived and born in sin and therefore are a child of wrath by nature, wholly incapable of doing any good, and prone to all evil; and that thou have frequently, in thought, word and deed, transgressed the commandments of the Lord: and whether thou are heartily sorry for these sins?

Answer. Yes.

Thirdly. Do thou believe that Christ, who is the true and eternal God, and very man, who took his human nature on him out of the flesh and blood of the Virgin Mary, is given thee of God, to be thy Saviour, and that thou does receive by this faith, remission of sins in his blood, and that thou are made by the power of the Holy Ghost, a member of Jesus Christ and his Church?

Answer. Yes.

Fourthly. Do thou assent to all the articles of the Christian religion, as they are taught here, in this Christian Church, according to the Word of God; and purpose steadfastly to continue in the same doctrine to the end of thy life; and also do thou reject all heresies and schisms, repugnant to this doctrine, and promise to persevere in the communion of the Christian

Church, not only in the hearing of the Word, but also in the use of the Lord's Supper?

Answer. Yes.

Fifthly. Has thou taken a firm resolution always to lead a Christian life; to forsake the world and its evil lusts, as is becoming the members of Christ and his Church; and to submit thyself to all Christian admonitions?

Answer. Yes.

The good and great God mercifully grant his grace and blessing to this thy purpose, through Jesus Christ Amen.

Thanksgiving

Almighty God and merciful Father, we thank and praise thee, that thou hast forgiven us and our children all our sins, through the blood of thy Son Jesus Christ, and received us through thy Holy Spirit, as members of thine only begotten Son, and adopted us to be thy children, and sealed and confirmed the same unto us by holy baptism. We beseech thee, through the same Son of thy love, that thou wilt be pleased always to govern this baptized person by thy Holy Spirit, that he may lead a christian and godly life, and increase and grow up in the Lord Jesus Christ, that he may acknowledge thy fatherly goodness and mercy, which thou hast shown to him and to us, and live in all righteousness, under our only Teacher, King, and High Priest, Jesus Christ; and that he may manfully fight against and overcome sin, the devil and his whole dominion, to the end that he may eternally praise and magnify thee, and thy Son Jesus Christ together with the Holy Ghost, the one only true God. Amen.

FORM FOR THE PUBLIC CONFESSION OF FAITH

(Before or after the sermon the minister requests those who intend to make public confession of their faith to arise and reply to the following questions:)

1. Do you acknowledge the doctrine of our church, which you have learned, heard, and confessed, to be the true and complete doctrine of salvation, conforming with the Sacred Scriptures?

2. Do you promise, by the grace of God, to continue steadfastly in the profession of this doctrine and to live and die in accordance therewith?

3. Do you promise, at all times to conduct yourself conformably to this doctrine, faithfully, honorably, and beyond reproach, and to adorn your confession with good works?

4. Do you promise that you with submit to admonition, correction, and church discipline in the event (which God forbid) that you may become delinquent either in doctrine or in life?

Answer: Yes.

FORM FOR THE PUBLIC CONFESSION OF GUILT

(Before or after the sermon, the minister requests those who intend to make public confession of their guilt to arise and reply to the following questions:)

1. Do you confess before God and His holy congregation that you have sinned against the ... commandment?

2. Do you acknowledge that this transgression grieves you?

3. Do you promise to forsake this sin and the world, and live in a Christian way in the future?

Answer: Yes.

FORM FOR THE ADMINISTRATION OF THE LORD'S SUPPER

BELOVED in the Lord Jesus Christ, attend to the words of the institution of the Holy Supper of our Lord Jesus Christ, as they are delivered by the holy Apostle Paul. 1 Cor. 11:23-30.

"For I have received of the Lord, that which also I delivered unto you, that the Lord Jesus, the same night in which he was betrayed, took bread; and when he had given thanks, he brake it, and said, Take, eat; this is my body which is broken for you, this do in remembrance of me. And after the same manner also, he took the cup, when he had supped, saying, This cup is the new testament in my blood; this do ye, as oft as ye drink it in remembrance of me; for as oft as ye eat this bread, and drink this cup, ye do show the Lord's death till he come. Wherefore, whosoever shall eat this bread, and drink this cup of the Lord unworthily, shall be guilty of the body and blood of the Lord. But let a man examine himself, and so let him eat of that bread, and drink of that cup; for he that eateth and drinketh unworthily, eateth and drinketh damnation to himself, not discerning the Lord's body.

That we may now celebrate the Supper of the Lord to our comfort, it is above all things necessary,

First. Rightly to examine ourselves.

Secondly. To direct it to that end for which Christ has ordained and instituted the same, namely, to his remembrance.

The true examination of ourselves consists of these three parts:

First. That every one consider by himself, his sins and the curse due to him for them, to the end that he may abhor and humble himself before God: considering that the wrath of God against sin is so great, that (rather than it should go unpunished) he has punished the same in his beloved Son Jesus Christ, with the bitter and shameful death of the cross.

Secondly. That every one examine his own heart, whether he does believe this faithful promise of God, that all his sins are forgiven him only for the sake of the passion and death of Jesus Christ, and that the perfect righteousness of Christ is imputed and freely given him as his own, yea, so perfectly, as if he had satisfied in his own person for all his sins, and fulfilled all righteousness.

Thirdly. That every one examine his own conscience, whether he purposes henceforth to show true thankfulness to God in his whole life, and to walk uprightly before him; as also, whether he has laid aside unfeignedly all enmity, hatred, and envy, and does firmly resolve hence forward to walk in true love and peace with his neighbour.

All those, then, who are thus disposed, God will certainly receive in mercy, and count them worthy partakers of the table of his Son Jesus Christ. On the contrary, those who do not feel this testimony in their hearts, eat and drink judgment to themselves.

Therefore, we also, according to the command of Christ and the Apostle Paul, admonish all those who are defiled with the following sins, to keep themselves from the table of the Lord, and declare to them that they have no part in the kingdom of

Christ; such as all idolaters, all those who invoke deceased saints, angels or other creatures; all those who worship images; all enchanters, diviners, charmers, and those who confide in such enchantments; all despisers of God, and of his Word, and of the holy sacraments: all blasphemers; all those who are given to raise discord, sects and mutiny in Church or State; all perjured persons; all those who are disobedient to their parents and superiors; all murderers, contentious persons, and those who live in hatred and envy against their neighbours; all adulterers, whoremongers, drunkards, thieves, usurers, robbers, gamesters, covetous, and all who lead offensive lives.

All these, while they continue in such sins, shall abstain from this meat (which Christ has ordained only for the faithful), lest their judgment and condemnation be made the heavier.

But this is not designed (dearly beloved brethren and sisters in the Lord), to deject the contrite hearts of the faithful, as if none might come to the supper of the Lord, but those who are without sin; for we do not come to this supper, to testify thereby that we are perfect and righteous in ourselves; but on the contrary, considering that we seek our life out of ourselves in Jesus Christ, we acknowledge that we lie in the midst of death; therefore, notwithstanding we feel many infirmities and miseries in ourselves, as namely, that we have not perfect faith, and that we do not give ourselves to serve God with that zeal as we are bound, but have daily to strive with the weakness of our faith, and the evil lusts of our flesh; yet, since we are (by the grace of the Holy Spirit) sorry for these weaknesses, and earnestly desirous to fight against our unbelief, and to live according to all the commandments of God: therefore we rest assured that no sin or infirmity, which still remains against our will, in us, can hinder us from being received of God in mercy, and from being made worthy partakers of this heavenly meat and drink.

Let us now also consider, to what end the Lord has instituted his Supper, namely, that we do it in remembrance of him. Now after this manner are we to remember him by it:

First. That we are confidently persuaded in our hearts, that our Lord Jesus Christ (according to the promises made to our forefathers in the Old Testament) was sent of the Father into the world; that he assumed our flesh and blood; that he bore for us the wrath of God (under which we should have perished everlastingly) from the beginning of his incarnation, to the end of his life upon earth; and that he has fulfilled, for us, all obedience to the divine law, and righteousness; especially, when the weight of our sins and the wrath of God pressed out of him the bloody sweat in the garden, where he was bound that we might be freed from our sins; that he afterwards suffered innumerable reproaches that we might never be confounded; that he was innocently condemned to death, that we might be acquitted at the judgment-seat of God; yea, that he suffered his blessed body to be nailed on the cross - that he might fix thereon the handwriting of our sins; and has also taken upon himself the curse due to us, that he might fill us with his blessings: and has humbled himself unto the deepest reproach and pains of hell, both in body and soul, on the tree of the cross, when he cried out with a loud voice, "My God, my God! why hast thou forsaken me?" that we might be accepted of God and never be forsaken of him: and finally confirmed with his death and shedding of his blood, the new and eternal testament, that covenant of grace and reconciliation when he said: "It is finished."

Secondly. And that we might firmly believe that we belong to this covenant of grace, the Lord Jesus Christ, in his last Supper, took bread, and when he had given thanks, he brake it, and gave it to his disciples and said, "Take, eat, this is my body which is broken for you, this do in remembrance of me; in like manner also after supper he took the cup, gave thanks and said, Drink ye all of it; this cup is the new testament in my blood, which is shed for you and for many, for the remission of sins, this do ye as often as ye drink it in remembrance of me": that is, as often as ye eat of this bread and drink of this cup, you shall thereby as by a sure remembrance and pledge, be admonished and assured of this my hearty love and faithfulness towards you; that, whereas you should otherwise have suffered eternal death, I have given my body to the death of the cross, and shed my blood for you and as certainly feed and nourish your hungry and thirsty souls with my crucified body, and shed blood, to ever lasting life, as this bread is broken before your eyes, and this cup is given to you, and you eat and drink the same with your mouth, in remembrance of me.

From this institution of the Holy Supper of our Lord Jesus Christ, we see that he directs our faith and trust to his perfect sacrifice (once offered on the cross) as to the only ground and foundation of our salvation, wherein he is become to our hungry and thirsty souls, the true meat and drink of life eternal. For by his death he has taken away the cause of our eternal death and misery, namely, sin, and obtained for us the quickening Spirit, that we by the same (who dwells in Christ as in the head, and in us as his members), might have true communion with him, and be made partakers of all his blessings, of life eternal, righteousness and glory.

Besides, that we by this same Spirit may also be united as members of one body in true brotherly love, as the holy Apostle says, "For we, being many, are one bread and one body; for we are all partakers of that one bread." For as out of many grains one meal is ground, and one bread baked, and out of many berries being pressed together, one wine flows, and mixes itself together, so shall we all, who by a true faith are in grafted into Christ, be altogether one body, through brotherly love, for Christ's sake, our beloved Saviour, who has so exceedingly loved us, and not only show this in word, but also in very deed towards one another.

Hereto assist us, the Almighty God and Father of our Lord Jesus Christ through his Holy Spirit. AMEN.

That we may obtain all this, let us humble ourselves before God, and with true faith implore his grace.

Prayer

O most merciful God and Father, we beseech thee, that Thou wilt be pleased in this Supper (in which we celebrate the glorious remembrance of the bitter death of thy beloved Son Jesus Christ) to work in our hearts through the Holy Spirit, that we may daily more and more with true confidence, give ourselves up unto thy Son Jesus Christ, that our afflicted and contrite hearts, through the power of the Holy Ghost, may be fed and comforted with his true body and blood; yea, with him, true God and man, that only heavenly bread; and that we may no longer live in our sins, but he in us, and we in him, and thus truly be made partakers of the new and everlasting covenant of grace. That we may not doubt but Thou wilt forever be our gracious Father, nevermore imputing our sins unto us, and providing us with all things necessary, as well for the body as the soul, as thy beloved children and heirs; grant us also thy grace, that we may take up our cross cheerfully, deny ourselves, confess our Saviour, and in all tribulations, with uplifted heads expect our Lord Jesus Christ from heaven, where he will make our mortal bodies like unto his most glorious body, and take us unto him in eternity.

Our Father which is in heaven. Hallowed be thy name. Thy kingdom come. Thy will be done in earth, as it is in heaven. Give us this day our daily bread. And forgive us our debts, as we forgive our debtors. And lead us not into temptation, but deliver us from evil: For thine is the kingdom, and the power and the glory, for ever.

Strengthen us also by this Holy Supper in the catholic undoubted christian faith, whereof we make confession with our mouths and hearts, saying:

I believe in God the Father, Almighty, Maker of heaven and earth; and in Jesus Christ his only Son our Lord; who was conceived by the Holy Ghost, born of the virgin Mary, suffered under Pontius Pilate, was crucified, dead and buried, he descended into hell: the third day he rose again from the dead, he ascended into heaven, and sits at the right hand of God the Father Almighty; from thence he shall come to judge the quick and the dead.

I believe in the Holy Ghost; I believe a holy catholic church; the communion of saints; the forgiveness of sins; the resurrection of the body; and the life everlasting. Amen.

That we may be now fed with the true heavenly bread, Christ Jesus, let us not cleave with our hearts unto the external bread and wine, but lift them up on high in heaven, where Christ Jesus is our Advocate, at the right hand of his heavenly Father, whither all the articles of our faith lead us; not doubting, but we shall as certainly be fed and refreshed in our souls through the working of the Holy Ghost, with his body and blood, as we receive the holy bread and wine in remembrance of him.

In breaking and distributing the bread, the Minister shall say:

The bread which we break, is the communion of the body of Christ.

And when he gives the cup:

The cup of blessing, which we bless, is the communion of the blood of Christ.

(During the communion, there shall or may be devoutly sung, a psalm, or some chapter read, in remembrance of the death of Christ, as the 53rd chapter of Isaiah, the 13th, 14th, 15th, 16th, 17th, and 18th chapters of John, or the like.)

After the Communion the Minister shall say:

Beloved in the Lord, since the Lord has now fed our souls at this table, let us therefore jointly praise his holy name with thanksgiving, and every one say in his heart, thus:

Bless the Lord, O my soul; and all that is within me, bless his holy name.

Bless the Lord, O my soul, and forget not all his benefits.

Who forgives all thine iniquities; who heals all thy diseases.

Who redeems thy life from destruction, who crowns thee with loving kindness and tinder mercies.

The Lord is merciful and gracious, slow to anger and plenteous in mercy.

He has not dealt with us after our sins, nor rewarded us according to our iniquities.

For as the heaven is high above the earth, so great is his mercy towards them that fear him.

As far as the East is from the West, so far has he removed our transgressions from us.

Like as a father pities his children, so the Lord pities them that fear him.

Who has not spared his own Son, but delivered him up for us all, and given us all things with him. Therefore God commends therewith his love towards us, in that while we were yet sinners, Christ died for us; much more then, being now justified in his blood, we shall be saved from wrath through him: for, if, when we were enemies, we were reconciled to God by the death of his Son; much more being reconciled, we shall be saved by his life. Therefore shall my mouth and heart show forth the praise of the Lord from this time forth forever more. AMEN.

Let every one say with an attentive heart:

Thanksgiving

O! Almighty, merciful God and Father, we render thee most humble and hearty thanks, that Thou hast of thy infinite mercy, given us thine only begotten Son, for a Mediator and a sacrifice for our sins, and to be our meat and drink unto life eternal, and that Thou give us lively faith, whereby we are made partakers of such great benefits. Thou hast also been pleased, that thy beloved Son Jesus Christ should institute and ordain his Holy Supper for the confirmation of the same. Grant, we beseech thee, O faithful God and Father, that through the operation of thy Holy Spirit, the commemoration of the death of our Lord Jesus Christ may tend to the daily increase of our faith, and saving fellowship with him, through Jesus Christ thy Son, in whose name we conclude our prayers, saying: Our Father which is in heaven. Hallowed be thy name. Thy kingdom come. Thy will be done in earth, as it is in heaven. Give us this day our daily bread. And forgive us our debts, as we forgive our debtors. And lead us not into temptation, but deliver us from evil: For thine is the kingdom, and the power and the glory, for ever. Amen.

FORM OF EXCOMMUNICATION

BELOVED in the Lord Jesus Christ; it is known unto you, that we have several times, and by several methods declared unto you the great sin committed, and the heinous offense given by our fellow-member , to the end that he, by your christian admonition and prayers to God, might be brought to repentance, and so be freed from the bonds of the devil (by whom he is held captive), and recovered by the will of the Lord. But we cannot conceal from you, with great sorrow, that no one has yet appeared before us, who has in the least given us to understand that he, by the frequent admonitions given him, (as well in private as before witnesses, and in the presence of many), is come to any remorse for his sins, or has shown the least token of true repentance. Since then he daily aggravates his sin, (which in itself is not small), by his stubbornness, and since we have signified unto you the last time, that in case he did not repent, after such patience shown him by the Church, we should be under the disagreeable necessity of being further grieved for him, and come to the last remedy; wherefore we at this present are necessitated to proceed to this excommunication according to the command and charge given us by God in his holy Word; to the end that he may hereby be made (if possible) ashamed of his sins, and likewise that we may not by this rotten and as yet incurable member, put the whole body of the Church in danger, and that God's name may not be blasphemed.

Therefore we, the ministers and rulers of the Church of God, being here assembled in the name and authority of our Lord Jesus Christ, declare before you all, that for the aforesaid reasons we have excommunicated, and by these, do excommunicate from the Church of God, and from fellowship with Christ, and the holy sacraments, and from all the spiritual blessings and benefits, which God promises to and bestows upon his Church, so long as he obstinately and impenitently persists in his sins, and is therefore to be accounted by you as a heathen man and a publican, according to the command of Christ (Matt. 18), who says, that whatsoever his ministers bind on earth, shall be bound in heaven.

Further we exhort you, beloved Christians, to keep no company with him, that he may be ashamed; yet count him not as an enemy, but at all times admonish him as you would a brother. In the meantime let every one take warning by this and such like examples; to fear the Lord, and diligently take heed unto himself, "If he thinketh he standeth, lest he fall"; but having true fellowship with the Father and his Son Jesus Christ, together with all faithful Christians, remain steadfast therein to the end, and so obtain eternal salvation. You have seen, beloved brethren and sisters, in what manner this our excommunicated brother has begun to fall, and by degrees is come to ruin; observe therefore, how subtle Satan is, to bring man to destruction, and to withdraw him from all salutary means of salvation: guard then, against the least beginnings of evil, "and laying aside," according to the exhortation of the apostle, "every weight and the sin which does so easily beset us, let us run with patience the race that is set before us, looking unto Jesus the author and finisher of our faith; be sober, watch and pray, lest you enter into temptation. Today, if you will hear the voice of the Lord, harden not your hearts, but work out your own salvation with fear and trembling;" and every one repent of his sins, lest our God humble us again and that we be obliged to bewail some one of you; but that you may with one accord, living in all godliness, be our crown and joy in the Lord.

Since it is God who works in us, both to will and to do of his good pleasure, let us call upon his holy name with confession of our sins, saying:

O! Righteous God and merciful Father, we bewail our sins before thy high majesty, and acknowledge that we have deserved the grief and sorrow caused unto us by the cutting off of this our late fellow-member; yea, we all deserve, should Thou enter into judgment with us, by reason of our great transgressions, to be cut off and banished from thy presence. - But O Lord, Thou art merciful unto us for Christ's sake; forgive us our trespasses, for we heartily repent of them, and daily work in our hearts a greater measure of sorrow for them; that we may, fearing thy judgments which thou executes against the stiffnecked, endeavour to please thee; grant us to avoid all pollution of the world, and those who are cut off from the communion of the Church, that we may not make ourselves partakers of their sins; and that he who is excommunicated may become ashamed of his sins; and since thou desires not the death of a sinner, but that he may repent and live, and the bosom of thy Church is always open for those, who turn away from their wickedness; we therefore humbly beseech thee, to kindle in our hearts a pious zeal, that we may labour, with good christian admonitions and examples, to bring again this excommunicated person on the right way, together with all those, who, through unbelief or dissoluteness of life, go astray.

Give thy blessing to our admonitions, that we may have reason thereby to rejoice again in him, for whom we must now mourn, and that thy holy name may be praised, through our Lord Jesus Christ, who has taught us to pray:

Our Father which is in heaven. Hallowed be thy name. Thy kingdom come. Thy will be done in earth, as it is in heaven. Give us this day our daily bread. And forgive us our debts, as we forgive our debtors. And lead us not into temptation, but deliver us from evil: For thine is the kingdom, and the power and the glory, for ever. Amen.

FORM OF READMITTING EXCOMMUNICATED PERSONS

BELOVED in the Lord, it is known to you, that some time ago our fellow member, was cut off from the Church of Christ; we cannot now conceal from you, that he, by the above mentioned remedy, as also by the means of good admonitions and your christian prayers, is come so far, that he is ashamed of his sins, praying us to be readmitted into the communion of the Church.

Since we, then, by virtues of the command of God, are in duty bound to receive such persons with joy, and it being necessary that good order should be used therein, we therefore give you to understand hereby, that we purpose to loose again the aforementioned excommunicated person from the bond of excommunication, the next time when by the grace of God we celebrate the Supper of the Lord, and receive him again into the communion of the Church; except any one of you, in the meantime, shall show just cause why this ought not to be done, of which you must give notice to us in due time. In the meantime, let every one thank the Lord, for the mercy shown this poor sinner, beseeching him to perfect his work in him to his eternal salvation. Amen.

Afterwards, if no impediment be alleged, the Minister shall proceed to the readmission of the excommunicated sinner, in the following manner:

Beloved Christians, we have the last time informed you of the repentance of our fellow-member to the end, that he might with your foreknowledge be again received into the Church of Christ: and whereas no one has alleged anything why his readmission ought not to take place, we therefore at present purpose to proceed to the same.

Our Lord Jesus Christ (Matt. 18), having confirmed the sentence of his Church, in the excommunicating of impenitent sinners, declares immediately thereupon, "that whatsoever his ministers shall loose on earth, shall be loosed in heaven"; whereby He gives to understand, that when any person is cut off from his Church, he is not deprived of all hopes of salvation; but can again be loosed from the bonds of condemnation. Therefore, since God declares in his word, that he takes no pleasure in the death of a sinner, but that he turn from his wickedness and live, so the church always hopes for the repentance of the backslidden sinner, and keeps her bosom open to receive the penitent; accordingly the apostle Paul (1 Cor. 5), commanded the Corinthian (whom he had declared ought to be cut off from the Church) to be again received and comforted, since being reproved by many, he was come to the knowledge of his sins: to the end that he should not be swallowed up with overmuch sorrow (2 Cor. 2).

Secondly. Christ teaches us in the aforementioned text, that the sentence of absolution, which is passed upon such a penitent sinner according to the Word of God, is counted sure and firm by the Lord; therefore, no one ought to doubt in the least, who truly repents, that he is assuredly received by God in mercy, as Christ says (John 20), "Whosesoever sins ye remit, they are remitted unto them."

But now to proceed to the matter in hand: I ask thee, whether thou do declare here with all thine heart before God and his Church; that thou are sincerely sorry for the sin and stubbornness, for which thou has been justly cut off from the Church?

Whether thou do also truly believe, that the Lord has forgiven thee, and does forgive thy sins for Christ's sake, and that thou therefore are desirous to be readmitted into the Church of Christ, promising henceforth to live in all godliness according to the command of the Lord?

Answer. Yes, verily.

Then the Minister shall further say:

We then, here assembled in the name and authority of the lord Jesus Christ, declare thee, to be absolved from the bonds of excommunication; and do receive thee again into the Church of the Lord, and declare unto thee that thou are in the communion of Christ and of the holy sacraments, and of all the spiritual blessings and benefits of God, which he promises to and bestows upon his Church: may the eternal God preserve thee therein to the end, through his only begotten Son Jesus Christ. Amen.

Be therefore assured in thy heart, my beloved brother, that the Lord has again received thee in mercy. Be diligent henceforward to guard thyself against the subtlety of Satan, and the wickedness of the world, to the end, that thou may not fall again into sin: love Christ, for many sins are forgiven thee.

And you, beloved Christians, receive this your brother, with hearty affection; be glad that he was dead and is alive, he was lost and is found; rejoice with the angels of heaven, over this sinner who repents: count him no longer as a stranger, but as a fellow-citizen with the saints, and of the household of God.

And whereas we can have no good of ourselves, let us, praising and magnifying the Lord Almighty, implore his mercy, saying:

Gracious God and Father, we thank thee through Jesus Christ, that thou hast been pleased to give this our fellow-brother repentance unto life, and us cause to rejoice in his conversion. We beseech thee, show him thy mercy, that he may become more and more assured in his mind of the remission of his sins, and that he may receive from thence inexpressible joy and delight, to serve thee. And whereas he has heretofore by his sins offended many, grant that he may, by his conversion, edify many. Grant also that he may steadfastly walk in thy ways to the end: and may we learn from this example, that with thee is mercy, that thou mayest be feared; and that we, counting him for our brother and coheir of life eternal, may jointly serve thee with filial fear and obedience all the days of our life, through Jesus Christ, our Lord, in whose name we thus conclude our prayer:

Our Father which is in heaven. Hallowed be thy name. Thy kingdom come. Thy will be done in earth, as it is in heaven. Give us this day our daily bread. And forgive us our debts, as we forgive our debtors. And lead us not into temptation, but deliver us from evil: For thine is the kingdom, and the power and the glory, for ever. Amen.

FORM OF ORDINATION OF THE MINISTERS OF GOD'S WORD

THE sermon and the usual prayers being finished, the Minister shall thus speak to the congregation:

Beloved brethren, it is known unto you, that we have, at three different times, published the name of our brother , here present, to learn whether any person had aught to offer concerning his doctrine or life, why he might not be ordained to the ministry of the Word. And whereas no one has appeared before us, who has alleged anything lawful against his person, we shall therefore at present, in the name of the Lord, proceed to his ordination; for which purpose, you , and all those who are here present, shall first attend to a short declaration taken from the word of God, touching the institution and the office of pastors and ministers of God's Word; where, in the first place, you are to observe, that God our heavenly Father, willing to call and gather a Church from amongst the corrupt race of men unto life eternal, does by a particular mark of his favour use the ministry of men therein.

Therefore, Paul says, that the Lord Jesus Christ has given some apostles and some prophets, and some evangelists, and some pastors and ministers; for the perfecting of the saints, for the work of the ministry, for the edifying of the body of Christ. Here we see that holy apostle among other things says that the pastoral office is an institution of Christ.

What this holy office enjoins, may easily be gathered from the very name itself; for as it is the duty of a common shepherd, to feed, guide, protect and rule the flock committed to his charge; so it is with regard to these spiritual shepherds, who are set over the Church, which God calls unto salvation, and counts as sheep of his pasture. The pasture, with which these sheep are fed, is nothing else but the preaching of the gospel, accompanied with prayer, and the administration of the holy sacraments; the same word of God is likewise the staff with which the flock is guided and ruled, consequently it is evident, that the office of pastors and ministers of God's word is,

First. That they faithfully explain to their flock, the Word of the Lord, revealed by the writings of the prophets and the apostles; and apply the same as well in general as in particular, to the edification of the hearers; instructing, admonishing, comforting and reproving, according to every one's need; preaching repentance towards God, and reconciliation with him through faith in Christ; and refuting with the Holy Scriptures, all schisms and heresies which are repugnant to the pure doctrine. All this is clearly signified to us in Holy Writ, for the Apostle Paul says, "that these labour in the Word"; and elsewhere he teaches, that this must be done "according to the measure or rule of faith"; he writes also, that a pastor "must hold fast and right divide the faithful and sincere word which is according to the doctrine": likewise, he that prophesieth (that is, preacheth God's Word), speaketh unto men to edification, and exhortation and comfort. In another place he proposes himself as a pattern to pastors, declaring that he has publicly, and from house to house, taught and testified repentance towards God, and faith towards our Lord Jesus Christ. But particularly we have a clear description of the office, and ministers of Gods Word (2 Cor. 5:18, 19, 20), where the apostle thus speaks, "And all things are of God, who has reconciled us to himself by Jesus Christ and has given to us (namely, to the apostles and pastors) the ministry of reconciliation; to wit, that God was in Christ reconciling the world unto himself, not imputing their trespasses unto them, and has committed unto us the word of reconciliation. Now then we are ambassadors for Christ as though God did beseech you by us we pray you in Christ's stead, be ye reconciled to God." Concerning the refutation of false doctrine, the same apostle says (Titus 1:9): "That a minister must hold fast the faithful Word of God, that he may be able by sound doctrine, both to exhort and convince the gainsayers."

Secondly. It is the office of the Ministers, publicly to call upon the name of the Lord in behalf of the whole congregation; for that which the apostles say, we will give ourselves continually to prayer and to the ministry of the word, is common to these pastors with the apostles; to which St. Paul alluding, thus speaks to Timothy: "I exhort therefore, that first of all supplications, prayers, intercessions, and giving of thanks be made for all men; for kings, and for all that are in authority," etc. (1 Tim. 2:1 and 2).

Thirdly. Their office is to administer the sacraments, which the Lord has instituted as seals of his grace: as is evident from the command given by Christ to the apostles, and in them to all pastors: "Baptize them in the name of the Father, and of the Son, and of the Holy Ghost." Likewise: "for I have received of the Lord, that which also I delivered unto you, that the Lord Jesus the same night in which he was betrayed," etc.

Finally, it is the duty of the Ministers of the Word, to keep the Church of God in good discipline, and to govern it in such a manner as the Lord has ordained; for Christ having spoken of the Christian discipline, says to his apostles, whatsoever ye shall bind on earth shall be bound in heaven. And Paul will have the ministers to know how to rule their own house, since they otherwise neither can provide for, nor rule the Church of God. This is the reason why the pastors are in Scripture called stewards of God, and bishops, that is, overseers and watchmen, for they have the oversight of the house of God, wherein they are conversant, to the end that everything may be transacted with good order and decency; and also to open and shut, with the keys of the kingdom of heaven, committed to them, according to the charge given them by God.

From these things may be learned what a glorious work the ministerial office is, since so great things are effected by it; yea, how highly necessary it is for man's salvation, which is also the reason why the Lord will have such an office always to remain. For Christ said when he sent forth his apostles to officiate in his holy function, Lo, I am always with you, even unto the end of the world; where we see his pleasure is, that this holy office (for the persons to whom he here speaks, could not live to the end of the world) should always be maintained on earth. And therefore Paul exhorts Timothy, to commit that which he had heard of him, to faithful men, who are able to teach others, and he also, having ordained Titus minister, further commanded him to ordain elders in every city. (Titus 1:5.)

Forasmuch, therefore as we, for the maintaining of this office in the Church of God, are now to ordain a new minister of the Word, and having sufficiently spoken of the office of such persons, therefore you , shall answer to the following questions, which shall be proposed to you, to the end that it may appear to all here present, that you are inclined to accept of this office as above described.

First. I ask thee, whether thou feelest in thy heart that thou art lawfully called of God's Church, and therefore of God himself, to this holy ministry?

Secondly. Whether thou dost believe the books of the Old and New Testament to be the only Word of God and the perfect doctrine unto salvation, and dost reject all doctrine repugnant thereto?

Thirdly. Whether thou dost promise faithfully to discharge thy office, according to the same doctrine as above described, and to adorn it with a godly life: also, to submit thyself, in case thou shouldest become delinquent either in life or doctrine, to ecclesiastical admonition, according to the public ordinance of the churches?

Answer. Yes, truly, with all my heart.

Then the Minister, who demanded those questions of him, while he and other Ministers who are present, shall lay their hands on his head, shall say:

God our heavenly Father, who has called thee to his holy ministry, enlighten thee with his Holy Spirit, strengthen thee with his hand, and so govern thee in thy ministry, that thou mayest decently and fruitfully walk therein, to the glory of his name, and the propagation of the kingdom of his Son Jesus Christ. Amen.

Then the Minister shall, from the pulpit, exhort the ordained Minister, and the congregation in the following manner:

"Take heed, therefore, beloved brother, and fellow-servant in Christ, unto thyself and to all the flock, over which the Holy Ghost has made thee overseer, to feed the Church of God which he has purchased with his own blood: love Christ and feed his sheep, taking the oversight of them not by constraint, but willingly; not for filthy lucre, but of a ready mind, neither as being lord over God's heritage, but an example to the flock. Be an example of believers, in word, in conversation, in charity, in spirit, in faith, in purity. Give attendance to reading, to exhortation, to doctrine. Neglect not the gift that is in thee, meditate upon those things, give thyself wholly to them, that thy profiting may appear to all; take heed to thy doctrine, and continue steadfast therein. Bear patiently all sufferings, and oppressions, as a good soldier of Jesus Christ, for in doing this thou shalt both save thyself and them that hear thee. And when the chief Shepherd shall appear, thou shalt receive a crown of glory that fadeth not away."

"And you likewise, beloved Christians, receive this your minister in the Lord with all gladness, 'and hold, such in reputation.' Remember that God himself through him speaketh unto and beseecheth you. Receive the Word which he, according to the Scripture, shall preach unto you, 'not as the word of man, but (as it is in truth) the Word of God.' Let the feet of those that preach the gospel of peace, and bring glad tidings of good things, be beautiful and pleasant unto you. Obey them that have the rule over you, and submit yourselves; for they watch for your souls, as they that must give account; that they may do it with joy, and not with grief: for that is unprofitable for you. If you do these things, it shall come to pass, that the peace of God shall enter into your houses, and that you who receive this man in the name of a prophet, shall receive a prophet's reward, and through his preaching, believing in Christ, shall through Christ, inherit life eternal."

Since no man is of himself fit for any of these things, let us call upon God with thanksgiving.

Merciful Father, we thank thee that it pleaseth thee by the ministry of men, to gather a Church to thyself unto life eternal, from amongst the lost children of men; we bless thee for so graciously providing the Church in this place with a faithful minister; we beseech thee to qualify him daily more and more by the Holy Spirit, for the ministry to which thou hast ordained and called him; enlighten his understanding to comprehend thy holy Word, and give him utterance, that he may boldly open his mouth, to make known and dispense the mysteries of the gospel. Endue him with wisdom and valour, to rule the people aright over which he is set, and to preserve them in christian peace, to the end that thy Church under his administration and by his good example, may increase in number and in virtue. Grant him courage to bear the difficult ties and troubles which he may meet with in his ministry, that being strengthened by the comfort of thy Spirit, he may remain steadfast to the end, and be received with all faithful servants into the joy of his master. Give thy grace also to this people and Church, that they may becomingly deport themselves towards this their minister; that they may acknowledge him to be sent of thee; that they may receive his doctrine with all reverence, and submit themselves to his exhortations. To the end that they may, by his word, believing in Christ, be made partakers of eternal life. Hear us, O Father, through thy beloved Son, who has taught us to pray:

Our Father which is in heaven. Hallowed be thy name. Thy kingdom come. Thy will be done in earth, as it is in heaven. Give us this day our daily bread. And forgive us our debts, as we forgive our debtors. And lead us not into temptation, but deliver us from evil: For thine is the kingdom, and the power and the glory, for ever. Amen.

FORM OF ORDINATION OF ELDERS AND DEACONS

WHEN ordained at the same time. But if they are ordained separately this form shall be used as occasion requires.

Beloved Christians, you know that we have several times published unto you the names of our brethren here present, who are chosen to the office of elders and deacons in this Church, to the end that we might know whether any person had aught to allege, why they should not be ordained in their respective offices; and whereas no one has appeared before us, who has alleged anything lawful against them, we shall therefore at present, in the name of the Lords proceed to their ordination.

But first, you, who are to be ordained, and all those who are here present, shall attend to a short declaration from the word of God concerning the institution and the office of elders and deacons.

Of the elders is to be observed, that the word elder or eldest (which is taken from the Old Testament, and signifies a person who is placed in an honorable office of government over others), is applied to two sorts of persons who minister in the Church of Jesus Christ: for the apostle says, "the elders that rule well, shall be counted worthy of double honour, especially they who labour in the Word and doctrine." Hence it is evident that there were two sorts of elders in the Apostolic Church, the former whereof did labour in the Word and doctrine, and the latter did not. The first were the ministers of the Word and pastors, who preached the gospel and administered the sacraments; but the others, who did not labour in the Word, and still did serve in the Church, bore a particular office, namely, they had the oversight of the Church, and ruled the same with the ministers of the Word. For Paul, Rom. chap. 12, having spoken of the ministry of the word, and also of the office of distribution or deaconship, speaks afterwards particularly of this office, saying, "he that ruleth let him do it with diligence"; likewise, in another place he counts government among the gifts and offices which God has instituted in the Church: 1 Cor. 12. Thus we see that these sorts of ministers are added to the others who preach the gospel, to aid and assist them, as in the Old Testament the common Levites were to the priests in the service of the tabernacle, in those things which they could not perform alone: notwithstanding the offices always remained distinct one from the other. Moreover, it is proper that such men should be joined to the ministers of the Word in the government of the Church, to the end, that thereby all tyranny and lording may be kept out of the Church of God, which may sooner creep in, when the government is placed in the hands of one alone, or of a very few. And thus the ministers of the Word, together with the elders, form a body or assembly, being as a council of the Church, representing the whole Church; to which Christ alludes when he says, "Tell the Church" which can in no wise be understood of all and every member of the Church in particular, but very properly of those who govern the Church, out of which they are chosen.

Therefore, in the first place, the office of elders is, together with the ministers of the Word, to take the oversight of the Church, which is committed to them, and diligently to look, whether every one properly deports himself in his confession and conversation; to admonish those who behave themselves disorderly, and to prevent, as much as possible, the sacraments from being profaned: also to act (according to the Christian discipline) against the impenitent, and to receive the penitent again into the bosom of the Church, as does not only appear from the above mentioned saying of Christ, but also from many other places of Holy Writ, as 1 Cor. chap. 5, and 2 Cor. chap. 2, that these things are not alone intrusted to one or two persons, but to many who are ordained thereto.

Secondly. Since the apostle enjoins, that all things shall be done decently and in order, amongst Christians, and that no other persons ought to serve in the Church of Christ, but those who are lawfully called according to the christian ordinance, therefore it is also the duty of the elders to pay regard to it, and in all occurrences, which relate to the welfare and good order of the Church, to be assistant with their good counsel and advice, to the ministers of the Word, yea, also to serve all Christians with advise and consolation.

Thirdly. It is also the duty particularly to have regard unto the doctrine and conversation of the ministers of the Word, to the end that all things may be directed to the edification of the Church; and that no strange doctrine be taught, according to that which we read, Acts 20, where the apostle exhorts to watch diligently against the wolves, which might come into the sheepfold of Christ; for the performance of which, the elders are in duty bound diligently to search the Word of God, and continually be meditating on the mysteries of faith.

Concerning the deacons: of the origin and institution of their office we may read, Acts 6, where we find that the apostles themselves did in the beginning serve the poor, "At whose feet was brought the price of the things that were sold: and distribution was made unto every man according as he had need. But afterwards, when a murmuring arose, because the widows of the Grecians were neglected in the daily ministrations" men were chosen (by the advice of the apostles who should make the service of the poor their peculiar business, to the end that the apostles might continually give themselves to prayer, and the ministry of the Word. And has been continued from that time forward in the Church, as appears from Rom. 12, where the apostle, speaking of this office, says, "he that giveth, let him do it with simplicity." And 1 Cor. 12:28 speaking of helps, he means those, who are appointed in the Church to help and assist the poor and indigent in time of need. From which passage we may easily gather, what the deacon's office is namely, that they in the first place collect and preserve with the greats fidelity and diligence, the alms and goods which are given to the poor: yea, to do their utmost endeavours, that many good means be procured for the relief of the poor.

The second part of their office consists in distribution wherein are not only required discretion and prudence to bestow the alms only on objects of charity, but also cheerfulness and simplicity to assist the poor with compassion and hearty affection: as the apostle requires, Rom., chap 12; and 2 Cor., chap. 9. For which end it is very beneficial, that they do not only administer relief to the poor and indigent with external gifts, but also with comfortable words from Scripture.

To the end therefore, beloved brethren, that every one may hear, that you are willing to take your respective offices upon you, ye shall answer to the following questions:

And in the first place I ask you, both elders and deacons, whether you do not feel in your hearts, that ye are lawfully called of God's Church, and consequently of God himself, to these your respective holy offices?

Secondly. Whether ye believe the books of the Old and New Testament to be the only Word of God, and the perfect doctrine of salvation, and do reject all doctrines repugnant thereto?

Thirdly. Whether ye promise, agreeably to said doctrine, faithfully, according to your ability, to discharge your respective offices, as they are here described? ye elders in the government of the Church together with the ministers of the Word; and ye deacons in the ministration to the poor? Do ye also jointly promise to walk in all godliness, and to submit yourself, in case ye should become remiss in your duty, to the admonition of the Church?

Upon which they shall answer: Yes.

Then the Minister shall say:

The Almighty God and Father, replenish you all with his grace, that ye may faithfully and fruitfully discharge your respective offices. Amen.

The Minister shall further exhort them, and the whole congregation, in the following manner:

Therefore, ye elders, be diligent in the government of the Church, which is committed to you, and the ministers of the Word. Be also, as watchmen over the house and city of God, faithful to admonish and to caution every one against his ruin; Take heed that purity of doctrine and godliness of life be maintained in the Church of God. And, ye deacons, be diligent in collecting the alms, prudent and cheerful in the distribution of the same: assist the oppressed, provide for the true widows and orphans, show liberality unto all men, but especially to the household of faith.

Be ye all with one accord faithful in your offices, and hold the mystery of the faith in a pure conscience, being good examples unto all the people. In so doing you will purchase to yourselves a good degree, and great boldness in the faith, which is in Christ Jesus, and hereafter enter into the joy of our Lord. On the other hand, beloved Christians, receive these men as the servants of God: count the elders that rule well worthy of double honour, give yourselves willingly to their inspection and government. Provide the deacons with good means to assist the indigent. Be charitable, ye rich, give liberally, and contribute willingly. And, ye poor, be poor in spirit, and deport yourselves respectfully towards your benefactors, be thankful to them, and avoid murmuring: follow Christ, for the food of your souls, but not for bread. "Let him that has stolen (or who has been burdensome to his neighbours) steal no more: but rather let him labour, working with his hands the things which are good, that he may give to him that needeth." Each of you, doing these things in your respective callings, shall receive of the Lord, the reward of righteousness. But since we are unable of ourselves, let us call upon the name of the Lord saying:

O Lord God and heavenly Father, we thank thee that it has pleased thee, for the better edification of thy Church, to ordain in it, besides the ministers of the Word, rulers and assistants, by whom thy Church may be preserved in peace and prosperity, and the indigent assisted; and that Thou hast at present granted us in this place, men, who are of good testimony, and we hope endowed with thy Spirit. We beseech thee, replenish them more and more with such gifts as are necessary, for them in their ministration; with the gifts of wisdom, courage, discretion, and benevolence, to the end that every one may, in his respective office, acquit himself as is becoming; the elders in taking diligent heed unto the doctrine and conversation, in keeping out the wolves from the sheepfold of thy beloved Son;

and in admonishing and reproving disorderly persons. In like manner, the deacons in carefully receiving, and liberally and prudently distributing of the alms to the poor, and in comforting them with thy holy Word. Give grace both to the elders and deacons, that they may persevere in their faithful labour, and never become weary by reason of any trouble, pain or persecution of the world. Grant also especially thy divine grace to this people, over whom they are placed, that they may willingly submit themselves to the good exhortations of the elders, counting them worthy of honour for their work's sake; give also unto the rich, liberal hearts towards the poor, and to the poor grateful hearts towards those who help and serve them; to the end that every one acquitting himself of his duty, thy holy name may thereby be magnified, and the kingdom of thy Son Jesus Christ, enlarged, in whose name we conclude our prayers, saying:

Our Father which is in heaven. Hallowed be thy name. Thy kingdom come. Thy will be done in earth, as it is in heaven. Give us this day our daily bread. And forgive us our debts, as we forgive our debtors. And lead us not into temptation, but deliver us from evil: For thine is the kingdom, and the power and the glory, for ever. Amen.

FORM FOR THE INSTALLATION OF PROFESSORS OF THEOLOGY

BELOVED brethren, it is known unto you that our brother in the holy ministry, has been called by our last Synod to the important office of professor of theology at our Theological Seminary. To our joy he has accepted this call and we are now assembled to install him in office. For which purpose we request thee, brother, to arise and to listen to that which belongs to this office, and is placed by the Lord and the Church in thy charge.

Since our God, who is rich in mercy, has chosen in his great love a Church unto himself for the inheritance of eternal life, and will gather this Church through his Spirit and Word to the fellowship of his Son, in the unity of true faith, and to the increase of the knowledge of his will, so it pleases him to call men by his Holy Spirit, who as ministers of the Word are to preach the glad tidings of salvation among those who already belong to the Church and among those outside, who are yet without the knowledge of God's ways.

The first messengers of peace in the days of the New Testament were immediately taught by our Lord Jesus Christ, and were by him personally trained and sent. After the outpouring of the Holy Spirit he gave them great diversities of extraordinary gifts and knowledge of the mysteries of salvation of sinners and the up building of saints. Because these extraordinary methods, however, lasted only as long as the Lord judged them to be necessary for the founding of his Church among the nations, the necessity was soon felt of training youths and men for the holy ministry under the ordinary dispensation of the Spirit by the regular methods of education. And this especially in virtue of what Paul wrote in 2 Tim. 2:2, "And the things which thou hast heard from me among many witnesses, the same commit thou to faithful men, who shall be able to teach others also." The Apostle here points to what he had himself done and what he required of his disciple Timothy.

In obedience to this apostolic direction this training was originally done by learned and capable overseers of the Church. Later the schools of Alexandria, Antioch, and other important cities were especially engaged in this work. And when towards the end of the middle ages and in the sixteenth and seventeenth centuries universities arose in various places, theology was not incorporated merely as a faculty with other faculties, but usually recognized as Queen of Sciences. This was the more easily done because the Church. both Roman Catholic and Protestant, exercised authority over or concerned itself with everything.

As long as a university is founded on the basis of Holy Scripture, accepts the confession of a certain denomination, and this denomination has part control in the appointing of professors of theology, it cannot be disapproved of that future ministers of the Word should receive their education at such an institution.

Since, however, Paul in Rom. 3:2 expressly declares that the Church of the Old Dispensation, and therefore also the Church of the New Dispensation, was given the special prerogative that to her were intrusted the oracles of God, it follows therefore that the Church has a divine mission to proclaim the word of God, to collect from the Word of God her standards of faith, to study theology according to these words, and further to advance what is in direct connection with this study.

Conscious of this calling our Church has also established a Theological School and called the reverend brother to devote his talents to this School.

In behalf of our Church the Curators charge thee, esteemed brother, with the task of instructing and establishing in the knowledge of God's Word the students who hope once to minister in his Church. Expound to them the mysteries of the faith; caution them in regard to the errors and heresies of the old, but especially of the new day; seek to explain how they not alone as teachers are to instruct but also as pastors are to shepherd the flock of the Lord. Assist in maintaining order and discipline among the disciples, that our Seminary may continue to enjoy the respect, the support, the appreciation, the love and the prayer of the Church. Be a good example to the students, that they may not only profit from thy learning, but also find in thee a living illustration of the power and practice of true godliness.

Be engaged in all of this according to the measure of the gifts God gave thee, in dependence on the Lord's help and the light of the Holy Spirit.

And that it may now publicly appear that thou, highly esteemed brother, art thus disposed, thou art to answer the following questions:

First. I ask thee, dost thou feel in thy heart that thou art lawfully called of God's Church and therefore of God himself to this office?

Secondly. Dost thou believe the books of the Old and New Testament to be the only Word of God? Dost thou reject all doctrine repugnant thereto, and dost thou accept the doctrinal standards of this Christian Church as the truest expression of the doctrine of salvation?

Thirdly. Dost thou promise faithfully to discharge thy office according to the same doctrine above described, and to adorn it with a godly life?

Fourthly. Dost thou promise to submit thyself, in case thou shouldest become delinquent, either in life or doctrine, to the ordinance of the Church, and if necessary, to Church discipline?

Answer: Yes, with all my heart.

FORM OR ORDINATION OF MISSIONARIES

BELOVED in our Lord and Saviour and all here present. It is known to you that our brother , called by the ... as missionary minister of the Word among the Heathen (Dispersed), (and recently examined by the Classis of ...) is now to be publicly ordained (installed) as missionary. We, therefore, request thee, beloved brother, to arise and to attend to a short declaration touching the office of missionary ministers of the Word.

Since our God, according to his infinite mercy, has chosen a Church unto everlasting life, and gathers it by his blessed gospel, out of every nation, and of all tribes and peoples and tongues, unto the fellowship of his Son, in unity of the true faith, therefore our risen Saviour has ordained an office and has called men, to carry the message of salvation to all peoples, commanding his apostles, and in them all lawful ministers of the Word: "Go ye into all the world, and preach the gospel to every creature." Mark 16:15. For he that ascended far above all the heavens, that he might fulfill all things, gave some to be apostles; and some prophets; and some evangelists; and some pastors and teachers; for the perfecting of the saints, unto the work of ministering, unto the building up of the body of Christ. And the Apostles, responding to this, went forth into the world declaring the whole counsel of God, particularly repentance, and remission of sins, through faith in Jesus Christ, testifying: "for God so loved the world, that He gave his only begotten Son, that whosoever believeth in Him should not perish, but have eternal life." John 3:16. "But all things are of God who reconciled us to himself through Christ, and gave unto us the ministry of reconciliation: to wit, that God was in Christ reconciling the world unto himself, not reckoning unto them their trespasses; and has committed unto us the word of reconciliation. We are ambassadors, therefore, on behalf of Christ, as though God were entreating by us: we beseech you on behalf of Christ, be ye reconciled to God." 2 Cor. 5.

Without this word of reconciliation, faith in Christ and consequently salvation, is and remains forever impossible, for Holy Scripture says, Acts 4:12: "And in none other is there salvation: for neither is there any other name under heaven, that is given among men, wherein we must be saved"; and elsewhere: Rom. 10:14, 15, 17: "How shall they believe in him of whom they have not heard? and how shall they hear without a preacher? and how shall they preach, except they be sent? So then, faith comes by hearing, and hearing by the Word of God."

Although all ministers of the Word have in common, that to them is committed the preaching of the Gospel, the administration of the Sacraments, the government of the Church, and the maintenance of christian discipline, yea, all, that, according to the Word of God belongs to the office of pastor and teacher: and although from the difference of field of labour no difference is resulting, concerning office, authority or dignity, since all possess the same mission, the same office and the same authority, yet not withstanding this, it is necessary that some labour in the congregations already established, while others are called and sent to preach the Gospel to those without, in order to bring them to Christ. And let each man abide in that calling wherein he was called by the Church of God and consequently by God himself and whereunto each has received gifts, until it pleases the Lord to lead him along a lawful way to a different field of labour.

Unto the Heathen

That unto the Heathen also these glad tidings must be brought appears plainly from Matt. 28:19, "Go ye therefore, and teach all nations, baptizing them in the name of the Father, and of the Son, and of the Holy Ghost; teaching them to observe all things whatsoever I have commanded you."

The same was revealed to Peter by showing him as it were a great sheet let down by four corners upon the earth, wherein were all manner of beasts, and thereupon commanding him to go down to the Gentile Cornelius, saying: "Arise, and get thee down, and go with them, nothing doubting; for I have sent them," Acts 10:20. Likewise he spoke to Paul in a vision in the temple: "Depart: for I will send thee forth far hence unto the Gentiles." Acts 22:21.

This divine charge was also carried out by the church of Antioch, when they, after fasting and prayer, laid their hands upon Barnabas and Saul and sent them away to preach the gospel also unto the Gentiles, Acts 13. And when they on their first missionary journey had arrived at Antioch in Pisidia they testified to the contradicting Jews: "Lo, we turn to the Gentiles. For so has the Lord commanded us, saying: I have set thee for a light of the Gentiles; that thou shouldest be for salvation unto the uttermost part of the earth."

And besides all this it is evident that the work of missions is the task of the Church since the Lord Jesus himself calls his Church the salt of the earth, and says: "Ye are the light of the world. A city on a hill cannot be hid. Neither do men light a lamp, and put it under the bushel, but on the stand." Matt. 5.

Unto the Dispersed

That unto the Dispersed also these glad tidings must be brought is plainly inferred from what God says in Ezekiel 34:11-16: "For thus saith the Lord God: Behold, I myself, even I, will search for my sheep, and will seek them out. As a shepherd seeketh out his flock in the day that he is among his sheep that are scattered abroad, so will I seek out my sheep; and I will deliver them out of all places whither they have been scattered in the cloudy and dark day. And I will bring them out from the peoples, and gather them from the countries, and will bring them into their own land; and I will feed them upon the mountains of Israel, by the watercourses, and in all the inhabited places of the country. I will feed them with good pasture, and upon the mountains of the height of Israel shall their fold be: there shall they lie down in a good fold, and on fat pasture shall they feed upon the mountains of Israel. I myself will feed my sheep, and I will cause them to lie down, saith the Lord God. I will seek that which was lost, and will bring again that which was driven away, and will bind up that which was broken, and will strengthen that which was sick. I will feed them in judgment."

That the Lord does this by means of his servants, is clearly shown by the way wherein God, in the same chapter, rebukes the unfaithful shepherds: "Neither have ye brought again that which was driven away," and expresses his holy indignation because: "My sheep wandered through all the mountains, and upon every high hill: yea, my sheep were scattered upon all the face of the earth; and there was none that did search or seek after them." Ezek. 34:4, 6.

The same also follows from the fact that Jesus who Himself was sent "to the lost sheep of the House of Israel," calls the Church the salt of the earth, while besides all this, the example of the Apostle Paul teaches us plainly that it is our high calling to bring the bread of life to our dispersed brethren after the flesh everywhere, and therefore certainly first of all in our own country, to gather them, if possible, as congregations of our Lord.

And since thou, beloved brother, are now called and are now being sent to labour among the Heathen (Dispersed), thou are to consider which important duties, are thereby devolving upon thee:

In the first place thou are to bring to their attention by all fit and lawful means, the glad tidings that Jesus Christ has come into the world to save sinners. All thine actions, thy speaking and thy silence, yea, all thine influence is to cooperate to recommend the gospel of Christ. Let thy conversation be without covetousness; abhor that which is evil; cleave to that which is good, that thou mayest be able to say with the Apostle Paul, 1 Cor. 9: 19, 22, 27: "For though I was free from all men I brought myself under bondage to all, that I might gain the more. ... I am become all things to all men, that I may by all means save some. I buffet my body, and bring it into bondage: lest by any means, after that I have preached to others, I myself should be rejected."

Secondly, thou are holden, if it pleases Gods to make thy work fruitful unto the gathering of a church, to administer the Sacrament of Holy Baptism according to the institution of the Lord and the requirement of the covenant.

Furthermore, thou are called wherever it is necessary and possible to ordain elders and deacons even as Paul charged Titus, chapter 1:5, saying; "For this cause left I thee in Crete, that thou shouldest set in order the things that were wanting, and appoint elders in every city, as I gave thee charge." But lay hands hastily on no man.

Moreover, there is committed unto thee, as minister of Christ and steward of the mysteries of God, the administering of the Holy Supper of the Lord according to the institution of Christ.

Besides this, there is commended unto thee the maintaining of christian discipline in the midst of the congregation, by faithful use of the keys of the Kingdom, as our Lord Jesus has spoken: "Go, show him his fault, between thee and him alone," etc. And afterwards: "Verily I say unto you, what things soever ye shall bind on earth, shall be bound in heaven."

And finally, beloved brother, be a faithful servant of Jesus Christ, and a careful shepherd of the flock. "Preach the Word, be urgent in season, out of season; reprove, rebuke, exhort, with all longsuffering and teaching, ... be an example to them that believe, in word, in manner of life, in love, in faith, in purity." ... "Give heed to reading, to exhortations, to teaching. Neglect not the gift that is in thee." ... "Be diligent in these things; give thyself wholly to them; that thy progress may be manifest unto all. Take heed to thyself, and to thy teaching. Continue in these things; for in doing this thou shalt save both thyself and them that hear thee." (2 Tim. 4:2 and 1 Tim. 4:12b, 16.)

And that now everyone present may hear, beloved brother, that thou art willing, and ready to undertake the ministry of the Word among the Heathen (Dispersed), thou art requested to answer sincerely the following questions:

First. I ask thee whether thou feelest in thy heart that thou art lawfully called of God's Church and therefore of God himself, to this holy ministry?

Secondly. Whether thou dost believe the books of the Old and New Testament to be the only Word of God, and the perfect doctrine unto salvation, and dost reject all doctrines repugnant thereto?

Thirdly. Whether thou dost promise faithfully to discharge thine office, according to the same doctrine as above described, and to adorn it with a godly life; also, to submit thyself, in case thou should become delinquent either in life or doctrine, to ecclesiastical admonition, according to the public ordinance of the churches?

Answer: Yes; truly, with all my heart.

Then the Minister, who demanded those questions of him, while he and other Ministers who are present, shall lay their hands on his head, shall say:

"Go then, beloved brother, and teach all nations, baptizing them in the name of the Father and of the Son, and of the Holy Ghost. God our heavenly Father, who has called thee to his holy ministry, enlighten thee with his Holy Spirit, strengthen thee with his hand and so govern thee in thy ministry, that thou mayest do gently and fruitfully walk therein, to the glory of his Name, and the propagation of the Kingdom of his Son Jesus Christ." Amen.

FORM FOR THE CONFIRMATION OF MARRIAGE BEFORE THE CHURCH

WHEREAS married persons are generally, by reason of sin, subject to many troubles and afflictions; to the end that you and, who desire to have your marriage bond publicly confirmed, here in the name of God, before this Church, may also be assured in your hearts of the certain assistance of God in your afflictions, hear therefore from the Word of God, how honorable the marriage state is, and that it is an institution of God, which is pleasing to him. Wherefore he also will (as he has promised) bless and assist the married persons, and on the contrary, judge and punish whoremongers and adulterers.

1. In the first place you are to know, that God our Father, after he had created heaven and earth, and all that in them is, made man in his own image and likeness, that he should have dominion over the beasts of the field, over the fish of the sea, and over the fowls of the air. And after he had created man, he said, "It is not good that man should be alone, I will make him a help meet for him. And the Lord caused a deep sleep to fall upon Adam, and he slept; and he took one of his ribs, and closed up the flesh instead thereof. And the rib which the Lord God had taken from man, made he a woman, and brought her unto the man. And Adam said, this is now bone of my bone, and flesh of any flesh: she shall be called woman, because she was taken out of man. Therefore shall a man leave his father, and his mother, and shall cleave unto his wife, and they two shall be one flesh." Therefore ye are not to doubt, but that the married state is pleasing to the Lord, since he made unto Adam his wife,

brought and gave her himself to him to be his wife; witnessing thereby that he does yet as with his hand bring unto every man his wife. For this lesson the Lord Jesus Christ did also highly honour it with his presence, gifts and miracles, in Cana of Galilee, to show thereby that this holy state ought to be kept honorably by all, and that he will aid and protect married persons, even when they are least deserving it.

But that you may live godly in this state, you must know the reasons, wherefore God has instituted the same. The first reason is, that each faithfully assist the other, in all things that belong to this life, and a better.

Secondly. That they bring up the children, which the Lord shall give them, in the true knowledge and fear of God, to his glory, and their salvation.

Thirdly. That each of them, avoiding all uncleanness and evil lusts, may live with a good and quiet conscience.

For, to avoid fornication, let every man have his own wife, and every woman her own husband; insomuch that all, who are come to their years, and have not the gift of continence, are bound by the command of God, to enter into the marriage state, with knowledge and consent of parents, or guardians and friends; so that the temple of God, which is our body, may not be defiled; for, whosoever defileth the temple of God, him shall God destroy.

2. Next, you are to know, how each is bound to behave respectively towards the other, according to the word of God.

First. You, who are the bridegroom, must know, that God has set you to be the head of your wife, that you, according to your ability, shall lead her with discretion; instructing, comforting, protecting her, as the head rules the body; yea, as Christ is the head, wisdom, consolation and assistance to his Church. Besides, you are to love your wife as your own body, as Christ has loved his Church: you shall not be bitter against her, but dwell with her as a man of understanding, giving honour to the wife as the weaker vessel, considering that ye are joint heirs of the grace of life, that your prayers be not hindered. And since it is God's command, "that the man shall eat his bread in the sweat of his face," therefore you are to labour diligently and faithfully, in the calling wherein God has set you, that you may maintain your household honestly, and likewise have something to give to the poor.

In like manner, must you, who are the bride, know how you are to carry yourself towards your husband, according to the Word of God. You are to love your lawful husband, to honour and fear him, as also to be obedient unto him, in all lawful things, as to your Lord, as the body is obedient to the head, and the Church to Christ. You shall not exercise any dominion over your husband, but be silent: for Adam was first created, and then Eve, to be a help to Adam; and after the fall, God said to Eve, and in her to all women, "your will shall be subject to your husband." You shall not resist this ordinance of God, but be obedient to the word of God, and follow the examples of godly women, who trusted in God, and were subject to their husbands; "as Sarah was obedient to Abraham, calling him her lord": you shall also be a help to your husband in all good and lawful things, looking to your family, and walking in all honesty and virtue, without worldly pride, that you may give an example to others of modesty.

Wherefore you and you , having now understood that God has instituted marriage, and what he commands you therein; are you willing thus to behave yourselves in this holy state, as you here do confess before this christian assembly, and desirous that you be confirmed in the same?

Answer. Yes.

Whereupon the Minister shall say:

I take you all, who are met here to witness, that there is brought no lawful impediment.

Further to the married persons.

Since then it is fit that you be furthered in this your work, the Lord God confirm your purpose, which he has given you; and your beginning be in the name of the Lord, who made heaven and earth.

Hereupon they shall join hands together, and the Minister speak first to the bridegroom.

Do you acknowledge here before God and this his holy Church, that you have taken, and do take to your lawful wife, here present, promising her never to forsake her; to love her faithfully, to maintain her, as a faithful and pious husband is bound to do to his lawful wife; that you will live homily with her; keeping faith and truth to her in all things according to the holy gospel?

Answer: Yes.

Afterwards to the bride.

Do you acknowledge here before God, and this his holy Church, that you have taken, and do take to your lawful husband, here present, promising to be obedient to him, to serve and assist him, never to forsake him, to live homily with him, keeping faith and truth to him in all things, as a pious and faithful wife is bound to her lawful husband according to the holy gospel?

Answer. Yes.

Then the Minister shall say:

The Father of all mercies, who of his grace has called you to this holy state of marriage, bind you in true love and faithfulness, and grant you his blessing. Amen.

Hear now from the Gospel, how firm the bond of marriage is, as described, Matt. 19:3-9:

"The Pharisees also came unto him, tempting him, and saying unto him, Is it lawful for a man to put away his wife for every cause? And he answered and said unto them, Have ye not read, that he which made them at the beginning made them male and female, and said, For this cause shall a man leave father and mother, and shall cleave to his wife: and they twain shall be one flesh? Wherefore they are no more twain, but one flesh. What therefore God has joined together, let not man put asunder. They say unto him, Why did Moses then command to give a writing of divorcement, and to put her away? He saith unto them, Moses because of the hardness of your hearts suffered you to put away your wives; but from the beginning it was not so. And I say unto you, Whosoever shall put away his wife, except it be for fornication, and shall marry another, committeth adultery: and whose marrieth her which is put away does commit adultery."

Believe these words of Christ, and be certain and assured, that your Lord God has joined you together in this holy state. You are therefore to receive whatever befalls you therein, with patience and thanksgiving, as from the hand of God, and thus all things will turn to your advantage and salvation. Amen

Prayer

Almighty God, Thou, who dost manifest thy goodness and wisdom in all thy works and ordinances; and from the beginning hast said, that it is not good that man be alone and therefore hast created him a help meet to be with him, and ordained that they who were two should be one, and who dost also punish all impurity; we pray thee, since Thou hast called and united these two persons in the holy state of marriage, that Thou wilt give them thy Holy Spirit, so that they in true love and firm faith may live holy according to thy divine will and resist all evil. Wilt Thou also bless them as Thou hast blessed the believing fathers, thy friends and faithful servants, Abraham, Isaac and Jacob; in order that they as coheirs of the covenant which Thou hast established with these fathers, may bring up their children, which Thou wilt be pleased to give them, in the fear of the Lord, to the honour of thy holy name, to the edification of thy Church and to the extension of the holy gospel. Hear us, Father of all mercy, for the sake of Jesus Christ, thy beloved Son, our Lord, in whose name we conclude our prayer:

Our Father which is in heaven. Hallowed be thy name. Thy kingdom come. Thy will be done in earth, as it is in heaven. Give us this day our daily bread. And forgive us our debts, as we forgive our debtors. And lead us not into temptation, but deliver us from evil: For thine is the kingdom, and the power and the glory, for ever. Amen.

Hearken now to the promise of God, from Psalm 128: "Blessed is every one that feareth the Lord, that walketh in his ways. For thou shalt eat the labour of thine hands: happy shalt thou be, and it shall be well with thee. Thy wife shall be as a fruitful vine by the sides of thine house; thy children like olive plants round about thy table. Behold, that thus shall the man be blessed that feareth the Lord. The Lord shall bless thee out of Zion: and thou shalt see the good of Jerusalem all the days of thy life; yea, thou shalt see thy children's children, and peace upon Israel." The Lord our God replenish you with his grace, and grant that ye may long live together in all godliness and holiness. Amen.

www.ingramcontent.com/pod-product-compliance
Lightning Source LLC
Chambersburg PA
CBHW051606010526
44119CB00056B/805